More Garden Varieties

More Garden Varieties

AN ANTHOLOGY OF POETRY

Introduction by Douglas Burnet Smith

Aya Press / The Mercury Press &
THE LEAGUE OF CANADIAN POETS
Stratford / Toronto

Copyright The League of Canadian Poets for the authors, 1989

No part of this publication may be reproduced in any form without the written permission of the publishers, with the exception of brief passages for review purposes.

Aya Press gratefully acknowledges the financial assistance of the Canada Council and the Ontario Arts Council.

Cover design: Daurio and Daurio
Production co-ordination: The Blue Pencil
Typesetting: The Beacon Herald, Stratford, Ontario
Printed in Canada

Canadian Cataloguing in Publication

Main entry under title: More garden varieties: an anthology of poetry

Co-published by the League of Canadian Poets.
ISBN 0-920544-67-3

1. Canadian poetry (English) — 20th century.*
2. Canadian poetry (English)— Competitions.*
I. League of Canadian Poets.

PS8279.M67 1989
C811'.54'08
C89-094631-0
PR9195.25.M67 1989

Aya Press/The Mercury Press
Box 1153, Station F
Toronto, Ontario
Canada M4Y 2T8

Box 446
Stratford, Ontario
Canada N5A 6T3

The League of Canadian Poets
24 Ryerson Avenue
Toronto, Ontario
Canada M5T 2P3

CONTENTS

DOUGLAS BURNET SMITH
   Introduction   8

ELISABETH HARVOR
   At the Horse Pavilion   11
   The Other Woman   12
   Letter to a Younger Man in Another Country   14

ELYSE YATES ST. GEORGE
   Blue Moon   15

PATRICIA YOUNG
   The Mad and Beautiful Mothers   16
   Sculpture   17

SUSAN GLICKMAN
   A November Eclogue   19

ARTHUR ADAMSON
   In Memoriam   21

GEORGE AMABILE
   7. Poached Grilse   22
   Bachelor Suite   22

ROD ANDERSON
   Venus Genetrix   25
   Old Pagoda   27
   The Free Trade Universe   28

JOHN BARTON
   Topographics   30
   Organizational Problems at the Personal Level   31
   Indian Graveyard, Gulf of Georgia, 1968   33

WALID BITAR
   Other Places to Be From   35

WILLIAM BONNELL
   Cottage Country   37
   Toronto   39
   The Great Detective   41

LESLEY-ANNE BOURNE
　It　43
　The Catastrophe　44

HEATHER CADSBY
　The Ways of a Woman　45
　Sumach: a mini-grammar　45

RON CHARACH
　Waterlines　47

PAUL CONNOLLY
　Ghetto　49

TONY COSIER
　Phoning My Father　51

FRANCIS DAVIS
　Not Thinking　53

CATHY FORD
　The Pregnant Woman Poem #3　54
　The Woman, Pregnant　54
　The Woman, Still Pregnant　55
　The Woman, Pregnant in Winter　56

DEBORAH FOULKS
　The Shape of a Hand　57

RICHARD HARRISON
　My Father's Body　58

CORNELIA HOOGLAND
　Construction Workers Eating Lunch　59
　Poem for My Husband　60

CLAUDE LIMAN
　Biking in Late September with My Two-Year Old Son　61

DAVID MANICOM
　Penates　62

NADINE MCINNIS
   Birth Mark   63

PATRICIA MCKENZIE-PORTER
   Intifada: The Uprising   65

ELIZABETH PHILIPS
   The First and Only Lesson Is Breathing   67

BARBARA RENDALL
   Little Accounts: Long Spring Weekend   68

ROBERT RICHARDS
   Maya X 20   69

EMILY SION
   Large White Bird on a Chinese Screen   70

DARKO R. SUVIN
   On/to Shushi   71

JOHN UNRAU
   Brother Dryhthelm of Melrose   73

BRIAN VANDERLIP
   Constructions   75

JOHN WEIER
   The Common Loon   76

PATIENCE WHEATLEY
   Skywatchers   78

DALE ZIEROTH
   Destroyer of Atmospheres   80

Introduction

Welcome to the second edition of the League of Canadian Poets' National Poetry Competition, *More Garden Varieties*. The League is delighted to have Aya Press co-publish the competition's fifty best poems and three award-winning poems.

This year's judges, Robert Kroetsch, P. K. Page and Phyllis Webb had an extremely tough time making their selections; so tough, in fact, that they decided to award three prizes of equal worth, and a special mention.

This year's prize-winners have written fascinating poems that, coincidentally, all concern children; or are concerned, lovingly, about children. Elisabeth Harvor's "At the Horse Pavilion" captures perfectly the parents' nightmare of a lost child. The panic of the mother, as she and her partner frantically search the pavilion for their little boy, calling for him desperately, fearing the worst and seeing it in "faces that could be startled into goodness," hearing it in the "evil sound of/ horsemen's applause,"— this panic is the emotional axiom for "the way the world is truly divided."

"Blue Moon," a prose-poem by Elyse Yates St. George, evokes the stark, primitive landscapes of magical realism. Here, "a child who can see with her skin," explores the "phosphorescent" world of her own back yard, where there are "flying fishes" and "Burgess squirrels" who hide nuts that become "small sculptured hearts." Patricia Young's poem "Sculpture" describes "all the ten year old girls in the world" from the point of view of the mothers who wonder what will become of them. As the girls gleefully sculpt the suds in their hair into amazing geometrical patterns, the mothers wonder "where in the world they will go from here." Are their soapy "helmuts and crowns" merely ornamental, or do they presage the armour these girls may very well need once they've left childhood?

Susan Glickman's poem, to which the judges awarded a special mention, is a touching elegy that memorializes her "comradeship" with the poet Robert Billings, who took his own life two years ago. It is a "valediction" which certainly does not forbid mourning, and presents a pastoral but "turbulent landscape" of suicide and sorrow.

It's uncanny, really, the number of poems here about children, or the parents of children, these children having become parents themselves and watching their parents grow old and die. Arthur Adamson, Tony Cosier, and Richard Harrison all wrote poems about their fathers. Harrison fondly remembers from his boyhood bathing with his father, Cosier talks to his father long distance, longingly, while Adamson remembers his father's "inner brightness" and sees him transformed, in death, "into the shape of a crow."

Cathy Ford's "The Woman, Pregnant" poems celebrate pregnancy and genealogy. Echoing Wordsworth's "Immortality Ode," she contemplates the mysterious origins of life, where the "comet child" comes into the world "trailing clouds of glory"— here the glory of grandmothers and "unborn language." Ron Charach's "Waterlines" echoes Young's "Sculpture" in its fear of what may befall his baby daughter. Claude Liman goes "Biking in Late September with My Two Year-Old Son," the boy tucked in a snuggly on his back, "laughing in this coasting wind," unaware of the dangers that are signalled by the "bonfires of men" flaring in the dim distance. "Sumach" is Heather Cadsby's linguistically-inspired prayer for her daughter; and the mother in John Barton's "Topographics" sends her globetrotting adult son love-letters and maps, and dreams his death at a "checkpoint in Beirut." In "Venus Genetrix," by Rod Anderson, a mother is horrified by one child's treatment of another. We are reminded that while we may come into the world innocent, we learn cruelty quickly.

And the knowledge of this cruelty, if not the experience of it, is always with us, especially at the most intimate of moments. Nadine McInnis, in "Birth Mark," depicts one of those moments beautifully, as she describes a woman's thoughts on loving a man, the sexual politics of the relationship. The cruelty that politics can produce, especially politics mixed with religion, is evidenced in Patricia McKenzie-Porter's "Intifada: The Uprising." The "waste" of the conflict is on both sides. There are "skulls tossed" aside by ideologies that have become the "slogans and hate" of a collective nightmare.

And yet, as if in defiance of this nightmare, many of the poems here portray a world that trembles with the stillness of an ancient Chinese painting. Indeed, Darko R. Suvin's "Shushi" meditations are a suite that calms, asks us to "take in the singing peony." It demonstrates the attraction that a simpler life holds for Canadian poets, as does Emily Sion's "Large White Bird on a Chinese Screen." George Amabile's "Poached Grilse" dispels the complexities of rules and regulations, of the "law" and our need to break it, and offers instead the simplicity of "what we need from the sea." "Little Accounts: Long Spring Weekend," by Barbara Rendall, also affirms these "moments of glad grace," as Yeats had them. John Weier in "the common loon," William Bonnell in "Cottage Country" and Patience Wheatley in "Skywatchers" make these moments quintessentially Canadian. Their descriptions of the natural world remind us of the work of the Group of Seven.

Walid Bitar shows us, however, that there are "Other Places to Be From," and other times as well. So does Robert Richards in "Maya X 20," where the Mexican setting drenches him in mescal and hallucinatory desire. In fact, one could make the case that all the poems in *More Garden Varieties* are about desire, in one way or another. And so the League of Canadian Poets offers you the desire of these poems, in the hope that they bring not a little pleasure.

— *Douglas Burnet Smith*

ELISABETH HARVOR

At the Horse Pavilion

We lost you once, at the Horse Pavilion,
on a day of snappy wind
beating five flags above that brilliant

nightmare green in the sun and beyond
prayer but ready to live on a diet of it
for the rest of our days, we ducked and

ran among faces made blank or tender by our
terror, so that we understood for the first time
that this was the way the world was truly divided:

into those faces that could be startled into
goodness, and those that could not, but none of
them worth anything at all to us except for what

they could tell us as we kept calling out to them
the only words left to us, *A little boy!*, and the
colours of the clothes you were wearing, while the

polished horses kept mindlessly
clearing gates that were hardships, but distant,
whitewashed, the hardships of others, and sounds

mocked us too, in that whinnied bright air— a
ring of faint surf, the civil, evil sound of
horsemen's applause, and we ran into each other and

ran back and ran through the stadium of stalls and
sick straw-smell and ran out into the sun of the
Pavilion's mud plaza and there you were, on

the other side of the soot track that led toward the
weeping green park, your eyes fixed without
flinching on the main doorway, waiting for us

to come out sometime before
dark and we fled to you, crying
your name and I could see in your eyes how hard

you'd been standing your ground against terror,
how long you'd been forbidding yourself to
invent us, as if in inventing us you'd have

lost all chance to see us come out to you, but
how brilliant you seemed, having saved yourself
from harm, you didn't know it, you turned your

face to the taut thigh of my skirt, not to cry, and
we walked that way, my hand
holding your head to me while I could have

sworn I could feel you inhaling what I was thinking
through the skirt's grass-engraved cotton:
Until this moment I never knew what love is.

The Other Woman

Everywhere everywhere tidal
squalor— the great old summer
mansions turned into clapboard
apparitions, the beach an oil-slicked
desert of bombed sand and driftwood.
But as your car noses its way
into the low grove of weeds ringing
the beach's salted sand collar
we can't wait to pay our respects
to the clean morning's burning
air. We tumble out, breathing it in,
and it right away snatches and skips
our words out to the sea.
"Does the sea ever get seasick?"
She is hanging between us, your

youngest daughter, her feet
jacked up into the swinging crouch
of a monkey. You say that it did once.
"It got too wild and it slapped
itself around and then it got seasuck."
Seasuck! She shrieks this, playing
the old clown-and-audience game of
father and daughter, then twists
her hands out of the perch
of our hands and butts her head hard
into my jeaned knee. "You go away now!

You!" she shrieks at me, sucking
all the breath out from under the heart
her smaller, more savage heart tells her
it is only wisdom to injure. Your eyes,
quick and dark for me, tell me it's only this:
the old triangle, or else she's sniffed
the taint of guilt in our tenderness
for her. Today she is wearing her little
navy peacoat with the admiral buttons
and lifts her knees high to stamp
her shining boots hard down into
hard sand. Now she reaches up with both hands
to grab your fist and swing from it,
crouched bell on a rope,

and you start to lope with her down
the long ruin of wet stones,
a one-man-merry-go-round, running
spinning as she keeps dipping
and rising: is the sea, is the horse,
is the child, is the rider,
while her triumphing screams are more
and more drowned out by the drowsy
smash of the cold ocean.

Letter to a Younger Man in Another Country

At the post office the only letter with
foreign stamps on it is from someone I don't know well,
alone in Greece for the summer. I feel
a flash of hatred for it, coming as it does

from the wrong country. On the way home I meet a young
mother, pushing her baby boy in a carriage. Unhappy,
I bend to praise him. They tolerate my sweet nothings,
but after I've released them and walked on I hear

a fierce maternal swish and the clack of wooden
bracelets as the mother lifts her baby to her
to console him for having suffered the ordeal
of being admired by a stranger. I did the same
once— picked up my babies with the same crow
of the heart (*My* baby! *Mine!*), but I shouldn't speak
to you of my long years as a mother, I should touch myself
with the clever wand of silence and turn ageless. The thing is,

I think about you all the time. I probably shouldn't tell you
this, either: every morning, walking out for the mail, I become
younger than you are. And walking back I am older than I hope
to be, ever, even if we end up together and happy.

ELYSE YATES ST. GEORGE

Blue Moon

For Mary

once in a blue moon comes a child who can see with her skin
and ears that coil of intestines scarlet gold and emerald
lying inside the pelvic bowl all phosphorescent as flying fishes
or oil on rainwater found on the path just after the corner store
and before the tree trunk with its smooth oval place that is a
door for Burgess squirrels who hide hickory nuts among the roots
so that the child will find the small sculptured hearts with
pointed tips sharp enough to prick the finger like a Godmother's
needle that sews back-and-forth fast or back-and-forth slow
according to her mood signaling whether it's safe for the child
to come close or retreat to the back yard and the black sky
filled with stars and fireflies that glow for only one night in
Summer when the air is so soft it feels like silk drawn along the
skin soothing her to sleep until the day comes back bringing
things that are not her own   things that come as hollow-flanked
cats to walk the garden wall at dusk thrashing their plumped-up
tails and caterwauling   rumps raised in heat making it hard to
see past them to the cool moon in her place as always

PATRICIA YOUNG

The Mad and Beautiful Mothers

We are the children of the fifties
with the mad and beautiful mothers.
In the forties they went to movies in toeless
high-heels, smoked cigarettes and danced
with Leslie Howard, their madness occurring
some time later.

Perhaps it struck the night we were born
or that day at the park, swinging from our knees
we slipped from the bars. After that,
clotheslines collapsed in every backyard,
and children fell through the air
like bombs in September.

We left for school
and they barricaded the doors
with livingroom furniture. Later,
we climbed in through basement windows,
twisted and jived to rock'n'roll
while upstairs our mothers
bent their heads over sinks,
unable to wash their hair.

We hid our mothers from our friends,
our friends from our mothers. Thunder
and lightning and some disappeared
into closets or hospitals from which they
never emerged. Perhaps madness first struck
on that flight from Amsterdam, London, Glasgow,
the cabin hot and crowded,
and rain seeping in.

We learned to shift our lives
around and through them where they sat
at the dining room table staring through doors
in the wallpaper for days at a time.
We are the children who survived
the fifties and their mothers, even
their conversations with God.

It has taken us years to forgive them
their madness, though they loved us
despite it. Years to go back
to the muggy afternoons
the whole world reeked of spice
and sweat and vinegar.

It is late August
and our mothers are in the kitchen
pickling beets and cucumbers.
Like fiends they are pickling
silver-skinned onions
and anything else
that gets in their way.

Sculpture

all the ten year old girls in the world are washing their
hair they are sudsing it up with soap that smells of green
apples they are kneeling in rivers and bathtubs and

glacial pools they are washing their blonde or black or
auburn hair sculpting the stuff into spikes and curls they
are laughing and calling their mothers from gardens or

books or the youngest child helmets and crowns whip
like cream on top of their heads all over the world
mothers are seeing their daughters as never before

thinking perhaps this is the last time these girls will be
perfect as long-stemmed lilies all arms and legs and
beautiful eyes the mothers are standing in doorways

or crouching on sand banks all over the world the sun
drops behind mountains or violet clouds and the mothers
turn back to their other concerns wondering about these

girls who rinse their hair not once but twice who step
from the water shaking their heads and smelling of
apples where in the world will they go from here.

SUSAN GLICKMAN

A November Eclogue

for Robert Billings

Surely this is the beginning place, this terrible mountain of water?
How beautiful and rare and how bitter
spoiled by your grief.
I never saw Niagara till after you died and now
can never visit it without revisiting your death.
So you are incorporate in this landscape, Bob,
in the large unconscious scenery of my land with its lakes and forests
just as you desired.

Drowned poet, your grave site's immaterial
for you will always be here, falling and falling
into the always unfulfilled river
the sunlight flickering on ice as on your glasses
masking the eyes' meaning, their perplexity and hidden rapids,
rapid dart of humour which if unmet
sank back quietly, extinguished,
without offering itself up in comradeship
without explanation.

You never explained anything, did you?
Making it into a joke, telling us you'd be "going away,"
reading the last case of Sherlock Holmes— setting us up
for such deep regret.
How could you be so crazy with pain
and nobody know?

Standing here now what I do know is the song
of the cataract, fierce pastoral you grew up with.
It is sublime, so pure; it promises one moment
of absolute identity
then absolution.
I hope you got it, that moment, before everything
shattered. The moment you listened for in the pauses
of your poems, the way you described Van Gogh

"listening for heartbeats   the wings of the
body in their hiding place..."

The word "heart" almost your signature, Bob,
in every poem. The way I repeat your name now
to conjure you back.
The way you conjured a turbulent landscape around you with a
couple of props (amber bottles
constantly pouring, cigarettes releasing fragrant mist
over the haunted terrain)
evoking that Niagara you've finally dissolved into
everywhere you went, a protective boundary between yourself
and those strangers, your friends.

You relied on such sustaining rituals.
I still have a stack of your letters in my desk
each bearing the same valediction, one I never heard
from anyone else
but counted on from you.
"All things," Bob, you always wished me
"All things."

It's too late now, but you know I wished you the same.

ARTHUR ADAMSON

In Memoriam

H.A., 1895-1984

when my father died no light streamed from his rib cage
nor was he the coffined effigy of wax I had dreamed
when I first knew I hated him at fifteen
he was nothing but the carcass of his long suffering
there he lay   a remnant of solid human folly
and what I would miss of him was not the old world
manners of Anglo-Ireland   his conservative politics
love of Scotch whiskey   high Anglicanism   elegant
Greek books he couldn't read   no   it was his inner
lightness   the trick for instance at the burial
in St. John's churchyard   the mourners at the family plot
where the venerable family dead lay untroubled   untroubling
and he was on the church tower in the shape of a crow

GEORGE AMABILE

7. Poached Grilse

What is the law, out here, where there's not another
boat in sight? We take what we need from the sea
as we've always done, each of us, privately
and if they won't rise to the bucktail's yellow feather
dancing from sixty yards of line, smothered
in foam, in the sun, for hours, then I'll go deep
with a spinner strung from illicit weights, creeping
through chuck, trolling two slack jigs for cover.

Hauling them in on the wire, half asleep
from the cold, I can see them as rainbows, firm & clean
with the hard shimmer of silver and polished stone.
But there's no sport in this. Chilled to the bone
I take one more for an old friend who has flown
thousands of miles with a great white from the Rhone.

Bachelor Suite

1.

Orange burlap
lampshade

on a tall
stem of brass.

2.

After the bars close
I stand in the street looking up

at the lamp-lit room, imagining
how it would feel to be home-

less and the glow
from the window, the desk, the neat row of books

begins to deepen
as if with the sweetness of words

like *shelter*, *comfort*, and *grace*
till the wind comes up off the river

roughing my hair, numbing my face.
Then I climb the worn carpeted stairs

and let myself in
for what?

3.

Beside the piano the lampshade
collects light from the dusty globe

and spills it
over my hands on the keys—

spirit milk, tarnished
by too many years in the same

life, a *motif* of descending minors.
In its wire cage, the exhaust fan

heavy metal
caricature

of a four-leaf clover, hums
and buzzes but refuses to sing.

4.

The unmade bed
this last light on the street

seems to offer *all*
the time in the world

(hazardous dream
common as failed ambition)

and I let my wrinkled fingers reach
odd harmonies that close

but can't resolve
the silence, wondering

as the snow begins
to sift through stiffened leaves

if trees will feel the cold
flakes

melt
the illusion of time

into the softer illusion
of timelessness

as chords build
and burn

temporary shelters
for the heart

whose first sleep
is always

waiting
in the dark

wings
of a song.

ROD ANDERSON

Venus Genetrix

Val has just run over Kate's finger,
wheeled her red tricycle back and forth,
methodical steamroller, squishing the small pink
wriggler securely into the garden mud.
I see it from the kitchen window, horrified,
come flying out like one of the Furies,
can't believe she's gone this far,
think of running over Val's hands with our Porsche,
send her to her room instead,
pick up Kate, who stops her bawling, wants to nurse,
afterwards burps mouthfuls over my shoulder,
I feel my blouse stick, soggy down my back,
wonder when Alan will be home.
In summer we used to make love on the beach.

Val is throwing things about her room,
Quickly I change Kate's diaper, put her into her carriage,
go up, tell Val for *godsake* to calm down,
her dolls are lying all over the floor,
stupid dolls, she says, I order her to pick them up,
she does so sulkily, sees that I'm about to blow,
two are already missing— out the window,
I shut her door angrily.
At the freshman dance I wore white (like a Venus, Alan whispered).

He phones me now to say he's taking
a New York customer to Winston's for dinner,
will be home late, (the last time we had people *here*
Val hid a frog in the caterer's oven,
it jumped about in frenzied whirls, never turned into prince,
ended its breathless ecstasy drowned in the souffle).
Kate's starting to cry again,
I go downstairs, pick her up, walk round the kitchen,
she falls asleep during the spin cycle,
I sneak with her up to her room,
lower her into her crib, gingerly, like docking a satellite,

her breathing pauses, starts up again,
miraculously her eyes stay closed,
I bring Val downstairs with me, my hand over her mouth,
whispering to her we'll play a game.
This morning our neighbours told me they're going overseas.

Val and I play fish with her new cards,
you've got threes, you've got threes, she squeals,
splashes laughter all over me when she wins,
hugs me, asks can she visit Marie next door,
it's too late, Marie's asleep, I say,
too chicken to tell her yet that Marie will be leaving,
can I stay till... ? no, I say, he'll be late,
then a story, OK, so I tell her about
a mermaid trying to ride a red tricycle,
Val smiles, kicks her legs in the air, I kiss her goodnight,
and for once she skips, gay as a woodnymph, off to bed,
I clean up the kitchen, harvest two broken dolls from the garden.
Next year I'm going to do something part-time.

I sip some coffee, look at real estate ads,
Alan comes in, slams the garage door, his eyes volcanic,
the customer didn't place the order,
he gets the Tanqueray gin from the freezer, the dark bottle
drops by mistake, shatters upon the anvil of our black tile floor,
haven't you had enough I ask, not you bloody too he shouts,
afterwards smiles apologetically,
sorry babe, he says, kisses my hand, I laugh,
we go upstairs, in bed he's all over me,
looks at me disgustedly when I don't come,
after he falls asleep I hold his head against my breasts,
stare out the window, a gibbous moon stares back.
Far off a tide turns, tugs at a large white shell.
I remember the clear light, the thighs of the young gods,
oceans of frenzied foam.

ROD ANDERSON

Old Pagoda

The universe was not created IN
space and time; space and time
are PART OF the created universe.
— *Paul Davies*

far away in a distant land under a banyan tree
lived the real universe
I mean it was really there
wherever *there* was and no fooling
and nothing else was there
because it filled up everything
oh maybe a peacock
                    or a golden pheasant
scratched nearby
but not right at that spot
where only the gilded galaxies spun
and had for billions of years
ever since— look who cares?— the point is
it lasted a long long time
and took up a lot of space
and that's what I mean by real

this makes the universe laugh
for it knows it was purely imaginary
made up its own space and time
then pulled itself into them
let there be bootstraps
and who was to argue?
the peacock and golden pheasant scratching nearby?
they weren't even recognized
I mean everyone knows the universe is an old solipsist
thinks nothing else exists—
more subtle still, existence:
an imaginary condition the universe dreamed up
to fit its own case

but dreams seed their own destruction
one day the universe fell asleep
and the instant its self-thinking stopped

why, its grasp gave way
space turned grainy   time crumbled into shards
and slumbering under the sacred aerial roots
the universe vanished and was never seen again

the peacock and the golden pheasant
scratch for seeds under the banyan tree
they imagine nothing
maybe the ruins of an old pagoda
one gilded finial gathering dust
nothing else

The Free-Trade Universe

if Canadians had designed the universe
don't laugh, I mean why couldn't they?
say, a couple of bright teen-agers one week-end at Waterloo
this crazy idea of a game, just a minute you ask
what sort of game? bingo for crowds of Acadians?
chess gambits for Bay Street?
a form of solitaire for Gastown?

look, I'm telling you, these are just kids
too naive to think of the market
they just invent this really neat game
with, you know, stars, planets, galaxies
a few simple rules
not a bad way to pass the time

but where'll they get enough energy to prime it?
(no such thing as a free launch)
of course they try the chartered banks
are told their scheme is too risky
they sell off the volatile parts
(black holes, super-nova explosions)
to Americans, who make a fortune on them,
finance the rest with Canada Council grants
provincial lotteries, distillery profits

and bang, off it goes!
at least for the first three seconds

which is when the NDP protest
planets are going to be unequally distributed
liberals steal their idea
set up a fund to buy two planets for every star
(there aren't enough to go around)
conservatives take over, keep the fund they pooh-poohed
but drop universality
bigger stars, after all, can support more planets
particularly conservative stars

provinces tell the feds: butt out, stars are regional
(they get their way finally and milk it)
somehow the Maritimes end up with the barren galaxies
Ontario grabs the richest cluster, running it prudently
for owners in New York
only annoyed at the fusion royalties to the west
townplanners travel to distant quasars
study conservation at the taxpayers' expense
Quebec renumbers its Messier objects in French

OK, it's easy to criticize, the place isn't bad
one can walk around the stars at night without being mugged
but who bothers?
I mean, where are we? a game from Canada?
folks just stick at home
wait for the Dallas model

JOHN BARTON

Topographics

Uncertain of his bearings his mother posts
him maps, shaking her head at this
child forever waylaid at some far-fetched
transfer point beyond her
womb: Winnipeg train station, Marrakech.

Though his letters hunger for brandied fruit cakes
tucked in foil, cushioned
for the journey in styrofoam chips
she cannot shake the image of an alien
body plumping a sleeping bag lost in New York.
Electric razors, cameras, hiking boots, a Seiko watch—
nearly every charm she gives him
he reports missing, phantom gifts elusive in pawn shops.

In a dream she sees his eyes blaze,
a suicide bomber exploding through a checkpoint in Beirut.
Waking, she almost gives up.

But maps furled in mailing tubes like semaphore flags...
her baby the centre
of some universe gravely unequipped
with parallels, sources, and marked barrier reefs.

The world she has surveyed for him
unscrolls across his desk.
The Queen Charlotte Islands list in a sea
of contour lines and quantified depths
before he folds the archipelago
against the creases she has tenderly ironed out,
the map stashed beneath letters
from the men he has loved, from the women.
Cancelled stamps are the only *Baedeker* he trusts.

It has taken him years to travel
blind, to move on touch and smell,
cities, like clams, freshest when dug up by chance.

He would prefer to remain helpless
in the wet jungle of some lover's legs and arms
but each river yet to be explored inside him
drains into a day he cannot remember,

the day his mother first let go,
infant feet flatfooting it down a zig-
zag path before he fell
ass-backward toward this world.

Organizational Problems at the Personal Level

This isn't the time to stare at the reflection
thrown back at her by the Frigidaire:
up all night, her hair (grey at 30) a frenzied maze.
She makes for the door, freeing purse and shoes
from eddies of shed work clothes
awash against the four walls of her studio.

The aroma of coffee is a mnemonic
that keeps her going.

At the corner she picks up a day-old *New York Times*
and the world unfolds
a bit off schedule: shots of the Queen kissing
babies in Beijing, bombs in Paris.
In a sunny cafe window she needn't care
if stocks fall on Wall Street
or if science can at last impregnate men.
Conception, she knows, is difficult no matter who you are,
the consequences more improbable if brought to term.
On an empty stomach she can't connect,
reads *Miss Manners* until the waiter fills her order.
She asks for an expresso, lights a cigarette,
knows the span of time it takes to burn

is the fuse eroding her
last moments of self-expression
before she takes off, explodes in late to work.

What matters are the nightly debates
recurrent over coffee with friends at Zak's.
Discussion isolates the exact
colour of ripe olives,
the fragrance of Montreal after a night of love,
the socio-economic debasement
of the tea ceremony in post-war Japan.

Experience fleshes out the essentials
variously now, no perspective
a consensus—
all that chic about being
and nothingness no longer in vogue,
absorbed in youth like vitamins
by the small intestine.

Somehow she remains unabashed,
strikes another match under one more
nonchalant cigarette, karmas
burning up as she tilts
her head back to laugh.

Walking home on moonless nights
she can't hide from herself,
conjures up rapists in ill-lit doorways,
her half-clad body pulled from the Rideau Canal.
Tubes and surgeons work into the night
like astronomers descrying signs
of life around some distant star.
Will they feel her drift further from them?
Will she sense no one ever really cared?
The result: negative patient care outcome,
the body unidentified at the morgue.

The catch is she has reasons to live
and these make her late for work.
It is the midnight calls from the man she loves
(long distance romance at 2/3's off costs her sleep);
the view of the river from her balcony
at dawn currents dragging
up memories of cocoa
with her dad after the graveyard shift.

Each morning she struggles, knows living for the moment
does not pay the rent.
On the down elevator to work, she's noticed her kind
gather around 9 AM; for them disorder
is not subsistence, these hesitantly dressed
men and women wanting coffee, their hair still wet.

Indian Graveyard, Gulf of Georgia, 1968

above in the cedars the bodies lie wrapped
in bark   beetles and rain
I cannot see them

other boys who risked the tricky
climb to each platform
flush with rumours of rags and grinning skulls
after supper   dusk and bones
of wood disappear into the smoke of the camp fire

we lie in a circle around the few embers

the sleeping boys I can see
are smiling   cold lips hardened
about ghost stories whispered moments ago
I did not hear them

wind like laughter climbs down through the trees

wave after wave repeats how we came
from one island over

stopping one night unlike those who stay
damp creeps into my toes and fingers

in the distance the glow of Vancouver
falters under the night sky as it swells
with constellations wheeling like goshawks

WALID BITAR

Other Places to Be From

From a ship full of rivers
others have mapped, it's possible to stare

at a sunny day's crowd,

even if no one
in it has a shadow, whether

or not there are native
bullets too
small to see in the air, there

are alligators that freeze

like aisles in a store. After

all, Da Gama discovered that Hindus

were Christians: "saints are painted
on the walls of the churches...

their teeth stick out one inch
from their mouths... they've got four
or five arms," he'd say, not knowing

his own planet might be an et-
cetera dot in some bigger language whose
users traded their appearances for

its disappearance. The missing glass

of a mirror some archaeologist finds,
that's your skin you look

into with a two
thousand B.C. expectation. It's
never as familiar as a face,

any face, even

Simon Signole's, a quattrocento
traveller sure a giraffe was almost
like an ostrich except

for its chest (which had no feathers), and

its horse's feet,
bird's legs,
ram's horns. That giraffe

probably escaped
after the men
pitched their voices like tents

and their songs left the night

out in the open.

WILLIAM BONNELL

Cottage Country

In the Beginning...
Those early mornings,
Spiritus Sancti,
the hush of an early mass:
the grate would creak
in the metal stove,
paper rustled
under dry kindling,
someone poured water
into a tin basin,
lingering smoke
replaced the faintly
mothballish odour
of an eiderdown,
you heard the drone
of a mosquito
and turned over
on your pillow.

The day wore on.
Sounds were only
briefly intrusive,
a hiatus,
like the shuffle of feet
on the stone floors
of old cathedrals:
the slap of the screen door,
the squirrel's burst
of staccato chatter,
the shrill insistence
of the cicada—
all suspended,
in the still heat
of the afternoon,
even the whine
of an outboard

on the lake
receding,
the water
quietly rocking the dock
back to silence.

And those evenings
on the porch
with its incense
of old shellac
and citronella,
its back copies
of Reader's Digest,
as worn as a scriptures,
the faint hiss
of a Coleman lantern,
the fugitive ululation
of a loon.

Cottage country.
At dawn the lake
always seemed
to be still asleep,
a clear, unbroken yolk,
unborn, clinging to itself alone,
waiting for no one.

Unfathomable, infatuate heart,
your enduring ache
for that silence,
that emptiness,
Genesis postponed
your longed-for redemption.

WILLIAM BONNELL

Toronto

One must say something—
what must one say about Toronto?
          — Rupert Brooke
      Letters from America

Wary of guards
I mounted a stone camel,
the recumbent pride
of some forgotten Khan,
then gawked up at the Tyrannosaur,
his stunted forelimbs
and razored jaw,
peered at the glassed in display
of life size Indians,
patiently chipping
their flint arrowheads,
scraping animal pelts
with bone implements.

Later we rode on the subway.
I mulled over
the ungainly names
of the stations.
Blue sparks flew
in a tunnel
darker than a mineshaft.
Passengers were rigid, cold eyed,
as the stuffed record lake trout,
netted in Athabaska years ago,
now pegged to the Museum wall.

Oh Toronto, Toronto,
legendary Sodom and Gomorrah
of the unredeemable south,
bustling den of pickpockets,
stock brokers
and sneering taxi drivers,
blight of foreigners who lived
in crowded houses

WILLIAM BONNELL

with wooden back staircases
and wallpaper that smelled
of cabbage soup,
home to shifty eyed little men
who scalped hockey tickets
on College Street
and bankers in baggy grey suits—
those dough faced clones
of Mackenzie King
who ate their lunch
at the King Eddy
and had heart failure
shovelling out driveways
of dirty, suburban snow.

Thirty years on
I ride the subway
and Yonge remains
a hoof or organ
found in an immigrant
butcher's shop,
Bloor Street,
a bucket of floor polish,
Osgoode, a box
of shortbread,
Dundas, a broken sofa.

What history is not
both memory and myth?

My stone camel
has never moved an inch,
the Tyrannosaur
still has his eager grin,
the same Indian,
his beaver pelt to scrape,
the record trout,
the same, indifferent,
glaucous stare.

WILLIAM BONNELL

The Great Detective

Who are they?
Foreigners, the insane,
the desperate.
An Irish mathematical genius
gone berserk,
sly continentals
who all bear a curious resemblance
to the Kaiser.
Men from good families
who have returned from abroad
with large gambling debts
exotic poisons, snakes,
and cannibalistic pygmies.

The wreath
of blue smoke
curls above the armchair,
the silent violin is at rest
on the mantel next to a lithograph
of Reichenbach Falls,
the deerstalker
hangs on a peg,
the brown fog winds its way
through the darkened streets below.

So it's not us out there
creeping around in black capes
under the gas lamps,
cuffing the stunted urchins,
measuring up the casual women
who linger in the doorways.
We've got other things
to worry about.
How the scarf turned into a snake,
why the dog didn't bark
and the sheep were lame,
there was no blood
on the rails,

a red headed man was paid
to sit in an office
and scribble out long passages
of the Encyclopedia Britannica,
a jewel was found
in the giblets of a goose.

So it never really
is a question of who.
Evil retains its reassuringly
singular condition.
As for ourselves,
we remain the loyal subjects
of a deductive, philosopher king.
In fact, some night,
at wits end,
might even pen the note
that now rests
on the tea tray
by the armchair:

>   *Dear Holmes,*
>
>   *I will have you know that*
>   *I have exhausted all other*
>   *means at my disposal,*
>   *only you, kind sir...*

LESLEY-ANNE BOURNE

It

sometimes it is like a jagged blue comb of glass
across my skin
                              — Sharon Olds, *It*

When I was little I'd race
fast as I could to the edge,
braking my bike right before
that second no one gets twice.
The rocks below hated me
teasing, holding back
my body offered only to *there*. I
didn't want to do it, sometimes
I must have known this—
but the roar of
waves against rock,
water spraying where I shook
up above, ahead
simply achieved refuge. Once
I thought I'd found Nipissing's island
but rain kept it away. Looking still
I stood leaning on the damn bike
over my parents' last fight,
downpours clouding the view.
No island, or at least not there then
that day I needed one. I pushed the tire forward,
little hands on the handlebars certain
the bike would or
the rocks would or maybe, finally,
the embankment would
give out.
Sometimes when you enter me
we become that day—
my bicycle, red and new that year,
dangerous rocks from
those fighting times— if I screamed

would you know it's not what you've done, it is
the making and breaking of the world
at the same moment.

*the last two lines are by Sharon Olds

The Catastrophe

I have decided to tell you
what sound loss makes.
These last days
before your counted-on departure, violins
move through the rooms slowly
like fan-tailed tropical fish,
colours billowing
as easily as the near-summer wind.
The summer you will miss.
Men on the street inexplicably
look like you, their onyx eyes
full of leaving, whole symphonies
of a lover going away,
the closing of the opera,
the awaited denouement.
Their hands are just as bad—
open as if emptied right then
of a breast
or any warm flesh,
the palms' unfolding outcome is
the catastrophe of chance. We expected
the way the music moved
discordant and haunting
near the end, but just before
the crescendo, that moment
we can never take back,
did you hear
the soft branches arch
toward the cascading snow

but how can you answer me now

HEATHER CADSBY

Employing linguistic processes to arrive at a ghazal titled: The Ways of a Woman

She slips off a mossy log
and longs for a language of breathing water.

She shuts off her ephemera
and whites out the best of everything else.

Using leftover morphemes
she snaps into instant-on

says, I'm never very good at order
but I am sensitive to charges of obscurity.

If you apply the stress rule
it's easy to see why hers is a lexicon of asides.

And why, in absence
she can almost speak what she thought to say.

Like a place of articulation that takes your breath away
this remarkable thing: she loves.

Sumach: a mini-grammar

And all the sumachs on the hills
Have turned their green to red.
    — Wilfred Campbell
      Indian Summer

From green to red
like a chorus
a Christmas hymn
an October walk

And so my daughter, these words.
Observe this fruit that is thick
red and rich with seeds.

It is not pomegranate. It is rather
upright, firm and oblong. Another story.

                Sue/Mac
Two kinds of flowers on separate trees.
    a) She was searching for him and never knew.
    b) She had always loved him and never knew.
The leaf-scar is heart-shaped on the poison variety.

She said:
It is also phonetically realized as s u m ae k.
The only English word which says an H that isn't there.
Really, he said, are you sure?

I said, I hate this straggling thing
with its crown of crooked branches
and I hate the way it forgets its stem.
I tore off the fruit cones. One was full of earwigs.
He said, why do you keep pulling off the fruit?
A snake on the path outsmarted us— kept to itself.

Look. There's this dream I have to tell you.
What happened was I spoke words so hurtful
you curled into a fetus. A frond. Nothing
to do with sumach.

My daughter, last words.
Do not carry sumach in your bridal bouquet.
For some few persons, rashes may occur.
This is not a day to take further risks.

RON CHARACH

Waterlines

Holding his baby daughter
as she squirms and chortles
in the chest-high water
of the sheltered bay,
her softness up against
his tightening skin,
nothing is but the sound of waves
and others playing—

Soon he will re-enter
the Sunday-night blur
of red taillights
snaking back to metropolis.
Or stop off at midnight
at the burger assembly
waiting for the traffic to thin,
other families pulling in
in campers, their two-year olds
in trances, fathers
so weary they throw their carkeys
in the trashbin.

Back on the highway
he will watch her in the one-way mirror,
his darling little charge
in her custom seat, content
even as the deerfly bites start to pop up
and their backs feel like beef
under the cotton shirts.

Finally she gives in to sleep,
and will miss the final hour of the journey.
This dark, it is her father's
more than hers.
Hers is more a perfect skin

flawed only by vaccination,
though there is none
against what lurks
in the long cold waters.

PAUL CONNOLLY

Ghetto

Before the ruin there was lust.
I saw it through the dirty blinds.
There were girls kicking balls between
the rows of houses, climbing up
the hill, then disappearing in
the wink of an early sunrise.

Barely awake, I ran to join in;
but I was poor, and each step out
the door sank one foot deeper in
debt. Though black with it, I held out
just long enough to learn that green's
the colour used to shield the groin.

That's when the floor fell, ledge and wall
fell. Like stockbrokers to their death,
even the shadows fell, and left
light, like a burning sword whose butt
has made my street this toothless Adam
where vacant lots now grow like weeds.

The girls who wouldn't play with me
have moved to better neighbourhoods.
The broken panes they've left behind them,
the walls blemished with smoke, the cracked
bricks falling away, the paint blistered
by heat of my frustrated fire.

The thirty years between lie buried,
at city's expense, somewhere
anonymous, remote; till dark
comes, lowering my sunburned palm
to pick up hints a rich man drops
once he's appraised the real estate.

He says I'm beyond renovation,
and offers nothing in exchange
but charity whose cost reduces
my sex life to the empty street
I'm chased down by the thirty years
it's been since I touched a woman:

to see him snake up his wife's skirt,
to sting with what it will be like
to have only the memory
of girls at play embracing me
once I have fallen, out of breath,
into bed with maggots and dirt.

TONY COSIER

Phoning My Father

They have built around his property
So the deer come less often now.

I've seen the photo he clipped
From the paper. And the one
With their scuts slipping off
Through the leaves that he caught with a panic click.

For my dad collects photos
In heaps like a miser, loves them
Maybe too much.
Though who am I to say that,

I, who last night again had the dream
I have had for twenty three years
Of going back through trees up a river
Always upstream, always toward the source,

Who simply by closing my eyes
Can bring to my nostrils the scent
Of apples in a childhood cellar,
Sawdust in a bin, wet pods in a bowl,

Who when I put down the receiver
Click with a buzz through his voice
Hunch for some time in my chair
And think of him quiet and seated

Looking out through a mist of rain
(For it often rains in Qualicum)
Where his lawn comes down to his garden
(For he has often kept a garden)

And let the arms from the old baseball snapshots
Lift and fall to the popping of gloves,
Let the light ride a mile of sand and then blue
To a white line of mountains beyond,

Let the deer come so close to the window
The nearest reflects at an angle
In one tawny spot
And smudges the glass with its breath.

FRANCIS DAVIS

Not Thinking

I am sweeping, I am
not thinking of you.
Angling broom straws round
the stove, under the table,
pulling a straight handle
back to a bent thigh
are not acts of collection;
these crumbs do not
represent our history.
When the door swings,
dust drifts and shifts;
I do not examine this
reassembly; it is not
like remembering what
you said I said we said,
seeing it always just
a little differently,
scraping it over
the edge of a shovel-shaped
pan, shaking it out
knowing I have not
got all of it, there is
still a slight crunching
underfoot, new layers
building, so that I am
always half thinking not
of you but of sweeping.

CATHY FORD

The Pregnant Woman Poem #3

year of the comet child
her mother's mother saw
a flash, a star tail
farther, norther, deeper european

still singsonging the english language
as if it were a caress, or some kind of geography
a favourite granddaughter, circular loves crossing the water
a beautifully long fingered flawless hand

one vanity, against the cheek of a duplicate spirit
the fire god, no one fearing that, but celebrating
all her lives, birth day's coming
into the fourth generation

tiny dreams, tiny sperm upstream, sons and daughters,
how the women in this family look
quite alike, birth mothers, a lineage
comprehensible, knowing this unborn language, this child

will it come, *trailing clouds and glory?*

The Woman, Pregnant

we were also that poor, neither coloured nor crippled,
nothing special, just assumed to be, middle class
working, working, and everyone thought we could carry it, grief
the violences in the family that everyone we knew somehow had

we were also that poor
in some ways, still are, but never loved violence or loathed it
so that's one of the things we carry
for each other, in love, peace

the smooth bruise, one that never fades
on the cheek, or ripped flesh

even though we've never given way to each other
we agreed to that, and to all the holy scars, porcelainized

perhaps it is because, of all our parents' children
you and I meet quite accidentally
not where we always loved them best, but simply
the most simply among all the siblings we shared the wombs of, kicking, kicking

now I am alone in a city far from you
farther than you can see, farther than even you can see
blue white blue, even farther than the deep veins
the doctors always accuse me of

still you are with me here, even when in the dark I whisper
hush baby mommy loves you peace. Please. Won't you please?

The Woman, Still Pregnant

the egg on the lawn
under the snow, like a metaphor
whether or not the metaphor is dead
hatching under a white blanket

why not, a water birth, clear blue as deep sea tropical
haemorrhage, my brother the physician says, haemorrhage
shark, her nightmares scream, gonads never seen
we never prayed for anything but a perfect child

outside, the snow disappears slowly from around the ootheca
white as snow, smooth, ovoid
oh they said the child comes out wrinkled, as if old
not an egg at all, the sac blood red as ripe liver

you have to watch closely or they'll make you miss it
be attentive, this may only happen once, egg and dart work
they may someday make something out of the placenta
you leave it in the hands of sterility if you're not careful

in other cultures burying the bloody things
makes more sense, more perfect sense
hasn't it already held and held
and held like a shell around the future, if it meets death

will metaphor ever be the same, will the perfect word scrabble?

The Woman, Pregnant in Winter

poetes maudits
this she will remember
and arrange nothing
real memory is like that

unalterable unchangeable
and no child
would be stillborn ever for us
not when we feel this much

before death even came into the family
we knew how to love children
without experience, the heart is absolute
which is why you and

I have always been in danger
of dying suddenly
like a small bird feathered from south america
dying of heat, light, exhaustion, fear, lack of love

you cannot take a child in your arms, just once, can you?

DEBORAH FOULKS

The Shape of a Hand

Birds lined up on the wire
wait for some firing squad
sparrows in the Smithrite
work on discarded lettuce
from the corner cafe
something grey the
shape of a hand
A man hides behind
the back-fence to pee
when he walks away he
makes a flute out of his
fingers blows a high
mournful tune
In Safeway the
tender half-smile
of an older man
choosing grapes
his fingers move as if
he is making love
I think of my Father
think that therein lies
our immortality
the clouds with the
light under them
bedding down the
mountains

RICHARD HARRISON

My Father's Body

I bathed with him as a child,
his enormous limbs
the gentleness of his cock at rest
in the water. My father, naked,
and I was naked and small
in his silence.

All the things I knew too late:
how he slept with my mother,
how the scars came to his body.

Later, I saw him pale, almost white,
stretched out on the couch,
his human body as long as furniture,
as long as an animal,
the power to lift
me and the world around me
gone,
whitened with the death inside him
growing;

my father's body immense even in this quiet
like the home planet,
immense with all it had done.

CORNELIA HOOGLAND

Construction Workers Eating Lunch

Their smell is rain in red-plaid jackets,
galvanized nails, smoke and coffee, sweat.
And wood. Splints and chips
pitched from the skillsaw's tarty wail.
The nutty rouse of hardwoods,
the greensap where the nails sink in.

But it's the lunchbuckets,
the snap and flip as the carpenters undo
the catches, expose the white enamel sides
and wrapped packages, that unbinds in me
those early morning kitchens,
harsh light on metal tins of coffee,
cold linoleum under bare feet.

And their carelessness. The unbandaged
broken skin on hands tearing soft bread
out of waxed paper, and how fast
they bolt tuna sandwiches between gulps
of cream-pale coffee. Then, leaning
back on stacks of two by fours, tilt their heads,
blow smoke rings in the air.

Roughnecks. Six floors up they joist
danger. Wear their muscles
casually under baggy pants
and their hardhats cast shadows
on whorling faces; beards dark with energy.

There's always a new one. One
whose pouch, stiff on his hips,
hasn't yet left scars; who is learning
to dangle cigarettes from limp and bending fingers;
learning to seem as casual as if he never in his life
looked in a mirror.

I look for him, the one leaning
into the world from a door jamb.
The young man my mother cried for
when she threw out Dad's black metal lunchpail
saved all the suited years since his Barrow days;
the one coming to the girl-turned-wife
in the basement suite kitchen;
his open, slightly credulous face cutting
like a wolf-whistle clean through my dress.

Poem for My Husband

Not for effect do I say we kissed in the orchard.
Like the gardener who left
it to bramble, I abandoned us
in grade nine, on the way home
from catechism. The moon clung to our cheeks
like small white squares on paintings of apples.
We stood quietly for over twenty minutes,
unmoving, as if waiting for our limbs
     those small hard knobs of breasts growing out of me,
     that bright act of yours, like Moses' rod-turned-snake,
to grow and twist together like branches.
As if we could stand in the moonlight under the trees
our whole life, waiting for this to happen.
                                    And we are.

CLAUDE LIMAN

Biking in Late September with My Two-Year Old Son

All day from the saddle
I've unreeled these fall fields
with quick feet geared down slow.
How easy to pull our two weights,
watch the fish-bowl shadow
of my son's white helmet
slide safe through this landscape
of turning leaves. To churn
the hamster wheel with tired thighs
feels like resistance.

At the crest of our last hill
I stand on both pedals
to get wind on my chest,
lengthen our short coast down.
Spokes whir, gears click.
West, the sun spins on sprockets
through flaming treetops. East,

men bustle at chores below us
on a street of tidy yards.
We wobble slowly across the flat,
seeking a summer that will not topple.
I vow not to pedal or put a foot down.

At the divide of summer,
last sun hot on my back,
I stand on balanced pedals
but can not stop. Somehow
wheels find one more spin,
then another, another, rolling now,
crushing leaves in the gutter,
my unseen son behind me
laughing in this coasting wind
we fan faster and faster
as we plunge toward bonfires of men
down in that valley where we live.

DAVID MANICOM

Penates

I came to the farm just before morning.
Here is where hills are hulls of the greater ships
that can move this slowly, preserving weather.
The dead lie on their decks with loam faces
and broken attitudes watching erasure
of eyelids and the fine rigging of roots.
Here the wind is a deep current, cold, brutal
with the scents of season and forced breath.
When we were children I hid in the porch
       — the laths! coarse against my cheek—
and watched mother stay out in the garden
long after dark, tending its colourless petals
with the faint morse of her shears. At last
a shadow split from the columns of trees

and passed, hiding its face, red eyes turned
to the empty, intimate pastures.
Now you've become where all aversions stare.
Here is where love is kept and cannot escape.
What you were blind to, in this place is vision,
where the hulls, where the sheer fissures of sail—
Here you are free only to remain.

NADINE MCINNIS

Birth Mark

you say it is the shape of Antarctica
my birthmark
stretched over one hip
some outpost sends signals
your tongue   surfaces
nimble as a seal

but I hear too
the silences between us
dry valleys where no rain has fallen
in two million years
secrets thick as nightfall
in which each of us wanders alone
longing to hear another human voice

where is the magnetic pole we search for
our children stretching up between us
drift and lean toward
maturity   those far-off solar storms
unfelt by us

long after they are gone
I'll still be marked with streaks
ridges of mountains   uninhabited now
and an older mark too
the birthmark of all women
that stains the imaginations of men

just as easily
it could be seen otherwise
soothing shadow of the baobab tree
at high noon
the outline of a turtle
dragging herself back to the warm sea
relieved of her worry of eggs

your body's terrain changes daily
I am at home with your prickly surfaces
the bright grasslands of your dreams
where I can stretch out
as you arc over me   a rainbow
over a plain

let us inhabit any land
but this one   of whiteouts
islands of deception
you must chisel and blast and drag
yourself with ropes away from

a wind change   caprice of nature
binds you to me again

am I still so unknown?
expanse of chilly fissures
raucous calls of my voice wheeling around you
spine turned away in the long dark

exiled here with weather watchers
a few twisted life forms
hunched between rocks
I see you across distances
reclining with the lions under that baobab tree
although our bodies nudge in sleep
the slow drift of continents
together and apart

PATRICIA MCKENZIE-PORTER

Intifada: The Uprising

Too long a sacrifice
Can make a stone of the heart.
           — W.B. Yeats

Rain rests the hills and mutes
                          this Holy Land
though in the heat and dust of grieving
I forget that its gentling fall
nurtured roses even when cinemas
ran the first newsreels of dozers
                          shovelling dirt
and bodies into a mass grave.

Walking from the theatre
pavement glistening and numb
                          round the heart
was also last night in Tel Aviv

and this evening the cypresses
                          turned red
thrust their roots from the earth
to disgorge tangled bones— white cries
reminding that in Israel
where fear is a bright burning
hearts become stones.

Beneath wild cyclamen and anemones
beneath irrigation canals
and roses unfolding, the Negev stirs
grain upon unsettled grain
gathering in a jihad of dry mouths
yelling slogans and hate

and it is here where
duty and sleep revolve in a nightmare
of forced doors in smoking streets

                      I recognize
a face which could be my mother's
my daughter's or mine— the reflection
of our likeness printed clearly
in each pupil or in a child
thinly clutching a stick, eyes
on my back sharpened to a single point

— this too we have known we Jews
who could not hate our oppressors
but within a ruin of mirrors
hate our victims, our own stark image
                          trembling behind a door.

Amid walls set at angles of discord
my weariness is a montage of femurs
                          and tibias
frail shafts splintered, skulls tossed
staring empty when we stood staring
emptied but promising "Next year,
next year in Jerusalem... "

Sigh of pines and waste, waste the places
the inhospitable pitted place
where children, my daughter was bombed

her grave tear-wet, rain-wet
a rose alone growing.

ELIZABETH PHILIPS

The First and Only Lesson Is Breathing

I get no pay for the work I do.
A woman who makes love to women, I teach
appreciation of the female.
The first and only lesson is breathing
deeply our wild smell: stamen and pistil
in hot sun, rich forest floor; darkness.

Their priests detest and fear me— the women
miss church on my account.
Lying late in my bed they sing and sweat,
anointing my face with their juices.
They are easily instructed— they eat me up,
my body so like their own.

I work for the pleasure of their pleasure.
Like sleepwalkers in daylight, they come to me,
one at a time, to learn what they know.
                        And when they come,
the sins of the fathers are displaced
by the spirit returning. And their minds clear,
like the sky arching over us
in the solemn quiet of Sunday morning.

BARBARA RENDALL

Little Accounts: Long Spring Weekend

> Nothing much but grocery lists,
> and a little account of nearly
> every day.
>   — H.T.

Friday

Turning the cold earth to steep in the sun,
We translate the season to ourselves,
Growing warm, and marking an emerging code:
Patterns of green shoots surfacing,
Vines instinctively running toward the light,
Slow bees bearing the first burden of sweetness home—
Joy randomly breaking, beauty opening us.

Saturday

The scent of cold earth lingers, even as we touch,
Striking the strangest balance
Of flesh and hard philosophy, mortality and desire;

Yet that which is most us is always luminous with life,
Bright on each leaf and blade, and poised to blossom,
Re-created in the arc of every rhyme and consummation.

Sunday

The week's longest day, and oldest,
A brief pitch backward in time to pooled quiet,
And faint bells ringing from odd corners: still.
Knowing more than we know, we go
Looking for rhyme and completion, a little sheepishly,
Suspecting that knowing can never be that simple,
A direct line to clear light and bright sound;
Not a bolt of lightning striking the new-risen form,
But gradual light gathering, haloing to eloquence
The worn configurations we continually wake to.

ROBERT RICHARDS

Maya X 20

For Bill Hathaway

YES. Bugbee told me in Missoula.
I've been here before but now
This excitement this ghost dance power
Greens me drenched calm this moment of serene
MAYA OXACACA MAYO mescal night
NEON ZOCALO MODELO CINCO
                    QUARTO LOVE
I came back, I couldn't
            LEAVE
1 a.m. milk run from the coast of
Rainbow hamacas tepid jugo de naraña.
At 5 a.m. pink plastered sweat stick electric
Drunk. "Si tango un cochia". "Aqui manito".
I lied— You screen door voice of my
            DESIRE!
Like I'd never left, soft twenty
Staring from the fish bowl on the mantle years later
           MAYA
I hear what you meant to scream.
I can't stay
                HERE, warm my glass eye.

EMILY SION

Large White Bird on a Chinese Screen

I hear your feathers rustling, quivering
as you hold the river, the wind,
                            and the chrysanthemums in place.

The river bubbles the paint to break free,
The wind's face is turning lacquered purple,
The chrysanthemums craze the finish
                        to fold up their petals,

But your wings will not let them,
they are the source of the river
the mind of the wind,
the open fist of the flower

Flight is the name of this landscape.

DARKO R. SUVIN
On/to Shushi

1. Meditations in the Shinkansen

To arrange flowers and tea-cups, stunt
Small trees and goldfish, plant every
Miniscule nook on the hillside— not these the only
Matters of shaping tenacious life to be learned
From the Japanese, neither specially martial nor
Martians, after all, simply the purest feudals Earth has seen
From the great Mongols and Roland's horn at Roncesvalles.

Now the ties of parent and child last here one lifetime,
Husband and wife two, master and vassal three: how many
Uneasy lifelines then, O mistress, am I to be enfeoffed
To you?— you descending, O kami, for one week
To wed the nether lands; you who are my sister-
In-arms; you who have no use for a steadfast vassal
Yet masterfully bind me with a cruel friendship

I would not miss? Unless the desert swallows us
Both forever, in our next five lives perhaps you'll be
A gracious bonsai tree, and I a reddish goldfish
Swimming in circular contentment around and around
The pond your bent little branches curve back upon:
Like Narcissus, rooted by the bank.

2. Nostalgia Leading Nowhere

The voice was a night river flowing thru willow branches
the body an oriole singing in the wooded hills

her wild apple blossoms enmeshed the silver Moon
her generous peony held rank upon rank of rising Suns.

3. For Shushi's Birthday, on My Birthday

The lush & fragrant peony
sheds crimson petals

You have drifted away, in the heat of Summer
it's difficult to maintain a pied-a-terre in Utopia

Do you still sometimes take in the singing peony?
Whenever Spring comes, my old feelings return.

Do we still know each other? Wordless, we should.
While this Earth turns, & petals scatter.

I hope you have somebody who moves his mattress near
& deep into the moony night, at ease together,

Speaks of your work with you, loves your body
& mind— these diseased words— as I did,

As with bitter longing I do.

4. How Would Wen Ting-yun Put This

They clasped and cried out at the generous peonies
The meeting was short, the parting was long
Affairs of the heart, who can really grasp?
The Moon stays bright, blossoms fill the branches
mono no aware.

Notes on Japanese terms:
Shushi, a Buddhist dancer-mesmerist, also performer of Miracle plays; with long "u", sadness; *shushin*, obsession of the soul, if unsatisfied during one's lifetime returns after death to haunt the object of that passion; with long "u", devotee. *shinkansen*, the fast train Tokyo-Kyoto. *kami*, numinous being, goddess, Lady. *mono no aware*, (approximately) "the pathos of things".

JOHN UNRAU

Brother Dryhthelm of Melrose

I'm smitten by the picture of you
drawn in Bede's old book
submerged to your neck in the flooding Tweed
chanting prayers in the dark
while lesser monks snore in their cells above
then standing rigid in your rags
until they dry against the shrinking flesh;

he says you saw a vision so intense
of cold awaiting sinners after death
that in the midst of winter
with shards of ice swirling round
which you smashed out to make your prayer hole,
when wondering spectators asked
how you could bear the chill,
you answered simply, "I have known it colder."

Bede thinks you abandoned your old wife
to undertake these hardships solely from
considerations of eternal gain;
and doubtless too the abbey's corporate image
benefited from your feats, which broke
all records for this sort of thing
set by those Irish monks at Lindisfarne.

Such cynicism might satisfy
financiers and church historians,
but having grown up in Saskatchewan
and known the esoteric joys of winter
I find a more compelling explanation
beside the pool where you once prayed
to the soft calling of owls;

and, old sensualist, I cannot help
but raise my voice with yours tonight,
for I see you stand ecstatic in this

eddying coil of splintered stars,
your blood cooling, pulse slowing
to the chill of the great stream,
the drift of Orion across the January sky.

BRIAN VANDERLIP

Constructions

They are cementing into place
a shopping centre beside
my only window.
Men with brightly coloured hats
are banging at the round world
this round morning
and everything is turning
into straight lines.
Yellow and red balloon heads
float among gray columns.
November is quietly crushing
October light to rust and brown.
What are we alive for,
rock-breakers and makers,
wood-carvers and stackers?
One day's orbit is bigger
than we will ever be;
the blood knows it.
Walking to the bus
the wind curves at me,
curves and makes me cry.
The bright-heads are shouting
about bad weather coming,
fractured syllables leaping
from third storey abutments.
Here and there, a first wet kiss
from white winter
puckers at the earth and vanishes.
Then, for no particular reason
I remember your arms
and the round place in them
where I would stay.

JOHN WEIER

The Common Loon

A loon sits in the middle of the bay at Pointe
du Bois. Quiet and calm. Periodically, he
turns his head to preen the back feathers at
the base of his neck. He isn't going anywhere,
isn't swimming, just floating in the middle of
the bay at Pointe du Bois. Stretches his
wings. Flaps them five times, his breast
rising out of the water. Then settles back. A
solitary wait.

Now, he pushes his head under water as if to
dive. But doesn't. His head comes back up.
He floats quiet and calm. Preens the feathers
on his back, flaps his wings. It rains for a
while, quiet circles on the water. The wind
rises to form little waves. Nothing much
changes, just the weather. Sun, rain, wind.
Day and night.

On the west shore of the bay, a man and woman
sit in their little grey compact. They have
been here before, come here often to sit in
silence. They watch the loon, the trees, the
bay. Sun, rain, wind. Night and day. The
moon. It is raining.

The man and woman talk about the loon. He is
so quiet and calm. They watch as he turns his
head to arrange the feathers at the base of his
neck. He isn't swimming, just drifting in the
middle of the bay. Stretches his wings, flaps
five times as his breast rises above the water.
Drops his head again as if to dive, again
doesn't. The man wonders what he is doing.

JOHN WEIER

The man has children in the city. He sees them
on Sundays. Has been married once. He wonders
why the loon doesn't dive, fly to another part
of the river. The woman lives alone. She will
never marry. She thinks the loon should find a
mate.

The loon sits quiet and calm. What is he
waiting for? How can he wait so long? The
rain stops. The sun comes out. The loon
drifts in the middle of the bay at Pointe du
Bois. The man and woman get out to stand
beside the car. Their hands touch. They think
the loon must be lonely. They have never seen
anything lonelier.

PATIENCE WHEATLEY

Skywatchers

Yesterday at noon
the sun immediately overhead
I stood on a dark island
without shadow

The same sun blazes
three quarters to zenith
dangerous.

Binoculars, milar-covered,
show a dark orange ball
ruling the bleached blue sky.

A dent appears at the sun's edge:
the moon moves across the sun's face
swallowing light

constricting my throat
spurring me to bang drums and rattles
shout, sing
embrace my friends

while the last nail-paring of orange sun
dies in the flame
of a Diamond Ring.

Flares shoot
from the sun's corona
and the dark moon in front
bordered with crimson beads

White Venus, white Mercury
hang in the dark blue sky
one above one below
the extinguished sun.

PATIENCE WHEATLEY

With a conflagration
the sun starts out again.

We look at one another
silent
like Cortes' men.

DALE ZIEROTH

Destroyer of Atmospheres

...mighty and weighty,
one of the ancients
riding blue off the horizon.
Out of the Bible's back pages,
out of the parts left over
once the animals awoke from sleep
to discover thump in their chests,
the light touch of the god constantly
reminding them to whom
they owed allegiance.
How complex they became
and we came too
even more divinely convoluted:
the destroyer of atmospheres
has begat you, and all around
but rapidly disappearing
the shimmer of the burst that fell
upon the void
and sent women off to the wells.

Night vision was given
to a special few: owl and wolf,
hunters at the edge of the burgeoning.
When we huddle together,
arguing still how to
block off the cave, we can hear
night workers pull at the edges
of the scheme. This is the way
we have come to see things,

we who see
into the dark but cannot find
the spark that sets the conflagration
going. I nudge my neighbour,
anticipate my partner.
I listen for the wind that might mean

we are about to be recalled,
remodelled again to fit
what's mighty, weighty
too.

NOTES ON THE CONTRIBUTORS:

ARTHUR ADAMSON has published two volumes of poetry, *The Inside Animal* and *Passages of Winter* (both Turnstone Press). He teaches Creative Writing and Literature at the University of Manitoba.

GEORGE AMABILE is the author of five books, and the 1983 recipient of the CAA Medal for Poetry. His work has been published recently in *The Lyric Paragraph*, *Garden Varieties*, *Arc*, *Margin*, and *Prairie Fire*.

ROD ANDERSON left a career as a chartered accountant five years ago to write full time: poetry, short stories, reviews and opera libretti. He lives with his wife near Cobourg, Ontario.

JOHN BARTON was born and raised in Alberta. His third collection of poetry, *West of Darkness: A Portrait of Emily Carr*, won the 1988 Archibald Lampman Award for Poetry. He lives in Ottawa.

WALID BITAR was born in Beirut in 1961. His first collection of poems, *Maps with Moving Parts*, was published in 1988 by Brick Books.

WILLIAM BONNELL lived in England for several years and has had poetry published in a number of UK journals and anthologies. He is working on a novel set in China in the 1930s.

LESLEY-ANNE BOURNE was born in North Bay, Ontario. Her poems have appeared in *Grain*, *Event*, *Northward Journal*, *Arc*, *CVII* and *Toronto Life*.

HEATHER CADSBY is the author of two volumes of poetry: *Traditions* (Fiddlehead, 1981) and *Decoys* (Mosaic, 1988).

RON CHARACH is a practising psychiatrist when he is not writing poems. His collection *The Big Life Painting* was published by Quarry in 1987.

PAUL CONNOLLY is a graduate of the University of Western Ontario, and lives in London where he writes poems, plays and film scripts.

TONY COSIER teaches English at Confederation High School in Nepean, Ontario. His poetry and fiction have been published in literary magazines and anthologies internationally.

FRANCES DAVIS teaches English and Women's Studies at Vanier College, Montreal. She is co-organizer of a Poetry Reading Series at Librairie sur le Parc, and has published poetry, fiction, and reviews in Canadian magazines and anthologies.

CATHY FORD lives on Mayne Island, B.C. and is a poet and fictioniste. A member of the LCP and of West Coast Women & Words/les femmes et les mots, she is the author of eight books of poetry, including prose and long poems.

DEBORAH FOULKS is a Vancouver writer whose work has appeared in *Canadian Literature*, *CVII* and several anthologies, including *Garden Varieties*. She has recently completed a novel, *Recent and Remote Memories*.

SUSAN GLICKMAN is the author of three books of poetry: *Complicity* (1983), *The Power to Move* (1986) and the forthcoming *Henry Moore's Sheep* (all Signal Editions). She teaches English at the University of Toronto.

RICHARD HARRISON attended Trent University, where he taught Philosophy and Communications for the past eight years. He is the author of *Fathers Never Leave You (1987),* which won second place in the *Milton Acorn Memorial People's Poetry Award.*

ELISABETH HARVOR is the author of two collections of stories: *Women and Children* (Oberon) and *If Only We Could Drive like this Forever* (Penguin). Her poems have appeared in *Malahat, Saturday Night, Canadian Forum* and *The Antigonish Review.*

CORNELIA HOOGLAND's book of poetry, *The Wire-Thin Bride,* will be published by Turnstone in 1990. She has recently moved to Vancouver from Calgary.

CLAUDE LIMAN teaches at Lakehead University in Thunder Bay, Ontario. *Becoming My Father,* his second book of poetry, was published in 1988 by Caitlin Press. He spent 1988-89 on sabbatical leave in Seattle.

DAVID MANICOM's poems have appeared in many Canadian journals, as well as in the US and UK. His first collection, *Sense of Season,* was published by Porcepic in 1988. He lives in Aylmer, Quebec.

NADINE MCINNIS' first book of poems, *Shaking the Dreamland Tree* (Coteau) was released in 1986. This poem is from her second manuscript, *The Litmus Body,* which is nearing completion.

PATRICIA MCKENZIE-PORTER is the author of a children's adventure, *When an Osprey Sails* (Nimbus, 1984). She has published poems in literary magazines, including *Poetry Canada Review* and *Cross-Canada Writers' Magazine.* She lives in rural Nova Scotia.

ELIZABETH PHILIPS is a poet who lives in Saskatoon. A book of poems, *Time in a Green Country,* will be published by Coteau in 1990.

BARBARA RENDALL lives in Lumsden, Saskatchewan. She is a sessional lecturer in English at the University of Regina, and has published poems in a variety of magazines, including *Grain* and *The New Quarterly.* Her short fiction has appeared in *Redbook* and *Chatelaine.*

ROBERT RICHARDS considers himself a: student, teacher, musician, husband, father, child, traveller, laugher and visionary.

EMILY SION grew up in Cuba, Arizona and Boston, and graduated from Harvard. She has been in Canada for twenty-eight years, except for periods in Florence, Strasbourg, Princeton, Berkeley and Paris.

DARKO R. SUVIN professes literature and theatre at McGill University. He has published a book of verse, *The Long March* (Hounslow Press, 1984).

JOHN UNRAU is a native of Saskatchewan who now lives in Toronto. His poems have been published in or accepted recently by: *Garden Varieties, Wascana Review, Scrivener* and *The New Quarterly.*

BRIAN VANDERLIP's first book of poems, *What Happens to Memory,* was published by Netherlandic Press in 1989.

JOHN WEIER's first collection of poetry, *After the Revolution,* appeared in 1986; *Ride the Blue Roan* was released in 1988 (both Turnstone). He is currently working on a collection of short stories and on a children's book.

PATIENCE WHEATLEY has published two collections of poetry: *A Hinge of Spring* (1986) and *Good-bye to the Sugar Refinery* (1989; both Goose Lane Editions).

ELYSE YATES ST. GEORGE was born in Ontario and now lives in Saskatoon. Her visual art and poetry have appeared in art and literary publications, and her first book of poetry, *White Lions in the Afternoon*, was published by Coteau in 1987.

PATRICIA YOUNG lives and writes in Victoria, British Columbia. Her fourth collection of poems, *The Mad and Beautiful Mothers*, is forthcoming from Ragweed.

DALE ZIEROTH lives in North Vancouver, B.C., and teaches at Douglas College in New Westminster, where he edits the literary journal *Event*. He is the author of three books of poetry, most recently *When the Stones Fly Up* (Anansi, 1985).

Other fine books from Aya Press/The Mercury Press:

Vivid: Stories by Five Women
Figures in Paper Time: Fictions *Richard Truhlar*
1988: Selected Poems & Texts *Gerry Shikatani*
Love & Hunger: An Anthology of New Fiction
The Blue House *Lesley McAllister*
Ink and Strawberries: An Anthology of Quebec Women's Fiction
Hundred Proof Earth *Milton Acorn*
In England Now That Spring *bpNichol & Steve McCaffery*
Arcana for a Silent Voice *Peter Baltensperger*
Empty Sky Go on Unending *Marjory Smart*
White Light *Brian Dedora*

Please write for our complete catalogue:

Aya Press/The Mercury Press
Box 446
Stratford, Ontario
Canada
N5A 6T3